Third Eye Awakening

How to open your third eye, use the pineal gland, and enhance your psychic abilities!

Table Of Contents

Introduction 1

Chapter 1: The Third Eye Explained 2

Chapter 2: Things that Affect the Third Eye 9

Chapter 3: Opening the Third Eye 14

Chapter 4: How to Use Your Third Eye 23

Conclusion 28

Introduction

I want to thank you and congratulate you for downloading the book, "Third Eye Awakening".

This book contains helpful information about third eye awakening, what it is, and how to do it.

You will soon learn about the different psychic abilities, and how you can begin to develop them! Awakening your third eye refers to opening yourself up to the psychic world, and allowing your mind to receive psychic information!

This book will provide you the steps and strategies required to successfully awaken your third eye. This step by step process is detailed in this book, and will have you easily opening your third eye in no time!

Also provided are some activities you can do to practice and hone your psychic abilities. These practices aim to test and improve your psychic skills, so that they become more reliable and efficient.

Thanks again for downloading this book, I hope you enjoy it!

Chapter 1:
The Third Eye Explained

The powers of the third eye, what science has to say about it, and the location of the third eye in the brain.

Do you know someone who can see ghosts, read tarot cards, or know accurate information out of the blue? This person may say that he/she has a third eye that allows them to have these unique skills. It's not unusual to be envious and wonder why you don't have this extra eye. Your curiosity may have led you to research about third eye awakening and psychic abilities, so that you can figure out how to develop these skills yourself.

Many people think that having a third eye is inborn and only a few have it. They are mistaken: *everyone* has a third eye, but some people use it more strongly than others. This book will teach you how to use yours.

First things first, what is the third eye? According to Hinduism and Daoism, it is a chakra or energy center that bridges the physical with the non-physical. Many belief systems include duality, or the characteristic of having a physical and a non-physical component. Myths, religions, and mystical traditions talk about material and heavenly realms, supernatural beings existing alongside living creatures, souls inhabiting bodies, and different dimensions of existence. The third eye is considered as the bridge between these matter and spirit. Since the spiritual world transcends the limitations of the physical (such as time, distance, method, ability, and energy constraints), using the third eye can allow a person to do impossible things.

The Benefits of Having an Awakened Third Eye

The third eye is derived from the third eye or brow chakra. The bindi, a red dot marking the space between the eyebrows, signifies the third eye. Although the eye is associated with seeing, the third eye is not limited to the visual sense. It has the ability to receive information that can overlap with the other senses: hearing, feeling (tactile and emotional), smelling, and tasting. It can also come in the form of direct cognition or an abstract concept that's not associated with any of the senses.

Some of the capacities of an open third eye are the following:

- Clairvoyance – seeing things that can't be seen by the eyes (spirits, subtle energy, hidden objects, etc.)

- Remote viewing – seeing things or places far away from the viewer; can be used for finding missing objects or people

- Clairaudience – hearing things not normally heard (spirit voices, audible information, etc.)

- Clairolfaction – smelling fragrances or odors that are not physically present

- Clairgustance – tasting flavors without physically putting a substance on the tongue or smelling an actual scent in the air (smells and tastes are sometimes linked)

- Psychometry – Getting information from energy imprints on an object or place

- Clairsentience – Feeling the presence of the invisible

- Telepathy – Receiving and sending thoughts
- Empathy – Receiving and sending emotions
- Channeling – Communicating with the unseen and relaying information from beyond
- Mediumship – Letting an entity speak through one's self
- Lucid Dreaming – Controlling one's dream
- Astral Projection – Projecting one's soul or consciousness out of the body
- Retrocognition/Precognition – knowing what happened or will happen
- Prophecy – Foretelling the future
- Psychic Diagnosis – Diagnosing ailments without using ordinary means
- Psychic Healing – Healing through psychic ability

Science and the Third Eye

In philosophy, dualism asserts that the mind and the body are separate from each other. This is the opposite of materialism, which is the belief that the mind is a result of the brain and non-material things do not exist. Dualism allows for the existence of the soul and everything else that doesn't have a physical characteristic. It also supports the existence of psychic abilities, which are said to arise from a person's spirit (the root word of psychic is psyche, a Greek word for mind, consciousness, and life force/spirit).

So far, science has not yet accepted the existence of spirit because it is heavily based on materialism. As a consequence, many people who trust in science refuse to believe in psychic abilities – or anything spiritual for that matter – unless they witness it for themselves and have no other explanation for it.

There are some things that make it hard for science to accept the third eye:

Psychic phenomena are hard to test

It's difficult to replicate psychic experiences in a laboratory. Many of them happen unexpectedly (for example, seeing someone's ghost at the exact time of a person's death without knowing about the person's condition beforehand, or sending an important message to another person during distress) and the scenarios that accompany them can't be matched accurately in a research setting.

Some say that psychic abilities are strongest when there's a great need for them to function – especially if a person's normal senses are severely limited. It is unethical and difficult to provoke this urgency to force psychic abilities to manifest. However, it's possible to test simple criteria, such by remote viewing an object, psychically picking up telepathy-projected information, changing the random distribution of numbers, etc.

Psychic phenomena are subjective

Psychic phenomena mostly occur within a person's own consciousness – unless it has effects on material objects such as with telekinesis, pyrokinesis, and levitation. It's currently hard for a scientist to know what's inside the mind of a psychic or even a normal person. The individual must express what's going on in his/her thoughts for them to be recorded. What science can do, however, is do brain scans to know what brainwaves are active and what brain regions are functioning at any one point. These data are somewhat useful but limited, just as looking at a book and weighing it on a scale does not tell what is written inside it.

Psychic phenomena implies the existence of non-material realms

Practicing psychics consult with unseen guides, masters, angels, elementals, spirits of the departed, etc. They perceive subtle energy and work with them for healing, creating servitors, or casting spells. Science has not found evidence that they exist so they consider psychic abilities as dealing with delusions and hoaxes.

Anecdotes are hard to verify

Science does not accept anecdotes or testimonials as evidence that something is genuine. Psychic feats often occur without anyone recording it or measuring it somehow. Thus, even if many people insist that they happen, they are not taken very seriously by skeptics.

Psychic events can be explained by normal causes

Skeptics are fond of using Occam's razor to explain mysterious things – that is, they will find the simplest reasons to explain how a strange thing happened. For example, if a psychic happened to know details about the life of a person he/she has never met before, the skeptics will say that the psychic has done research about the individual, someone has given the information to the psychic, the psychic has done cold-reading (a trick to gather info through observations and eliciting responses) or it is a mere coincidence that the psychic is right. They assume that psychic abilities are non-existent or at least very rare. These two assumptions are false.

In spite of these limitations, psychic and paranormal phenomena are studied by parapsychology institutions all over the world. These organizations have devised methods so that these events can be tested, recorded, and analyzed. Parasychology is considered as a pseudo-science, meaning that it doesn't pass the standards of mainstream science. That doesn't stop people from taking parapsychological research seriously – especially because psychic abilities point to a bigger reality that we should discover and utilize.

It's likely that you have encountered psychics and you are sure that no trickery has happened. If you have gone to many reputable psychics and read parapsychology studies of credible organizations, you will be convinced by now that these abilities exist. You may also have experienced spontaneous psychic activities yourself, and want to know more about how to control them.

The Pineal Gland and the Third Eye

The third eye, as it is commonly understood, is invisible and immaterial. However, it is sometimes associated with a physical body part: the pineal gland.

The pineal gland is a tiny gland located in the middle of the brain. It is the only unpaired structure in there. Because of its central position and its singularity, the philosopher Rene Descartes (1596-1650) theorized that it is the seat of the soul and the organ that connects the mind to the body. Centuries later, the pineal gland was discovered to excrete substances that control many bodily functions. One of these is melatonin, a hormone that influences the wakefulness of a person, supports gonad development, and regulates the menstrual cycles of women. It may also help counteract illnesses such as cancer, ADHD, autism, fibromyalgia, and IBS. This in some ways confirms Rene Descartes' idea that the pineal gland governs the body.

This gland produces melatonin only in darkness. Because of this, people are encouraged to get adequate sleep in dark conditions. In fact, some studies link cancers and other health problems to low levels of melatonin in the body. Prolonged wakefulness and bright lights at night suppress the pineal gland and cause unpleasant side effects.

Going back to the association of this mysterious gland to the third eye, the pineal gland is the last to be studied among all the endocrine glands in the human body, so it's not yet thoroughly understood. One discovery about the pineal gland is that it secretes DMT, a vision-inducing substance active during dreams and mystical states.

The pineal gland has a similar structure as an eye, leading some to theorize that it used to be a working eye before humans developed two eyes. This also explains why melanin function is dependent on light. Some consider these characteristics as signs that the third eye and the pineal gland is one and the same – at least, on the physical level. According to them, the third eye may be a sensory organ for the non-physical dimensions, such as the physical eye is for the physical dimension.

Chapter 2:
Things that Affect the Third Eye

How the third eye works and factors that hinder and strengthen its powers

Understanding the third eye involves learning about brainwaves, the pineal gland, and the things that influence them.

Brainwave levels

The mind has many frequencies:

- Gamma waves (30-80 cycles per second) – brain hyperactivity, alertness, anxiety

- Beta waves (13-29 cycles per second) – normal wakefulness, focus on external environment

- Alpha waves (8-12 cycles per second) - mental and physical relaxation, psychic states, focus on internal states

- Theta waves (4-7 cycles per second) - deep meditation, dreaming, psychic states

- Delta waves (.5-3 cycles per second) – deep sleep, astral projection, out of body experiences

It has been observed in psychics that physical and mental relaxation is very important in accessing their paranormal (beyond normal) abilities. In clairvoyance, telepathy, and precognition tests, people who had more alpha and theta brainwave activity scored higher than those who had more rapid brainwaves. This led researchers to conclude that the relaxed but attentive state in the alpha or theta level is very conducive for ESP functioning.

The delta level is linked to unconsciousness, which some say is helpful for detaching the soul from the physical body. This is a very deep trance (.5-3 cps), with 0 cps signifying death. The slowness of brain activity may trigger the consciousness (which, according to dualism, is separate from the brain) to detach from its physical vehicle and enter the spiritual realm.

You don't need to be hooked to an EEG device to know that you have reached alpha or theta. You will know that you are in a psychic level when you are not forcing yourself to pay attention, your whole body is relaxed, your mind is not engrossed in something, and you are feeling calm. You might become aware of phantom images, sounds, and other sensations just like when you are about to sleep or during the first few minutes of waking up. This is the hypnagogic state – a state of mind that allows you to become conscious of psychic impressions.

Geomagnetic Activity

There are other studies linking natural and artificial geomagnetic activity (from the sun, moon, and induced electromagnetic fields) to psi. The results vary among studies, but generally, it was seen that weak geomagnetic activity favors psi while strong geomagnetic activity inhibits it. Researchers theorized that geomagnetic activity affects how the pineal gland excretes neurochemicals that support psi activity because the gland and the brain in general contain magnetite, but further investigation needs to be done to confirm that theory. Other than the effect to the pineal gland, geomagnetic fields are also postulated to carry and influence psi information, as well as alter the qualities of consciousness to enable it to affect matter via quantum processes.

You can do your own experiments for linking geomagnetic activity with psi. While practicing your third eye, record the moon phase and solar activity (sunspots, solar flares, etc.) You may notice that you're highly psychic or least psychic at certain conditions – pay attention to these so you'll know when you can expect your third eye to be at its strongest and weakest.

Emotions

Many psychic instructors say that negative emotions are harmful for psychic ability. They teach that the third eye chakra is a high frequency energy center that should not be contaminated by low frequency vibrations coming from feelings such as hate, depression, or fear. This may be true because strong emotions can activate brainwaves and raise them to the delta or gamma levels (non-psychic levels). This is why it's important to achieve emotional tranquility when attempting to use psi.

Also, emotions can bias the perception of psychic impressions, such as when an overly scared person senses ghosts all around him/her even if there are no paranormal entities present, or when an abused person regularly perceives scenes of abuse around him/her, even in a newly constructed environment that nobody else had entered before. Thus, it's important that you remain as calm and detached as you possibly can before you attempt to receive psi information.

Environmental distractions

Conspiracy theorists warn that many things in our lives are designed to keep us distracted and dumb so we can be easily manipulated by those in power: TV shows, movies, news, fads, songs, social media sites, and so on. If you notice that you are being overly distracted and weakened by something, try to avoid it. Doing so may improve your psychological well-being and allow you to be in control your thoughts – this will help you become more psychic.

Diet

Mystical traditions encourage vegetarianism for those who want to develop spiritually and psychically. According to some gurus, the meats of butchered animals contain low frequency energies because of the suffering they underwent. If you want to raise the quality of your energy body and your third eye chakra, consider going vegan. However, there are many meat-eaters who are highly psychic, so this teaching may not be true for everyone.

Some proponents of organic farming say that commercially grown food have chemicals that harm the pineal gland and the overall health of the body. Try eating organic produce; this may improve your health and your psi abilities.

Fluoride is a controversial ingredient that is added in the water supply in some locations to reduce cavities. There are people who say that fluoride damages the brain and the vital organs of the body, and the government is intentionally poisoning the population so that they will be easily controlled. The pineal gland in particular is potentially in danger of fluoride because this gland accumulates calcium deposits when it comes into contact with sodium fluoride. You may use reverse osmosis or distillation treatments for your water so that you can avoid drinking this questionable ingredient.

There are some psychic practitioners that say chocolate, coffee, and some kinds of tea (mugwort, cinnamon, lemongrass, damiana, star anise, and peppermint) encourage psychic expressions. Others rely on hallucinogens such as LSD, ayahuasca, and peyote. *You do not need these things to open your third eye.* When you develop your psychic faculties without relying on external substances, you will learn how to use it at will, anywhere and anytime.

Chapter 3:
Opening the Third Eye

Different ways to open the third eye and use psychic abilities

There are two general ways to awaken the third eye: by relaxation or by stimulation. These are normally done for about 20 minutes and longer for the adept.

Relaxation

As discussed in the previous chapter, deeply relaxed states are associated with psychic abilities. This is quite tricky because psychic functioning requires 'letting go' instead of straining to achieve something. Before moving on, it's useful to learn the difference between the ordinary mind and the psychic mind, or the conscious and subconscious.

The Conscious and Subconscious

The mind is made up of the conscious and the subconscious. The conscious mind is the part that includes normal awareness, short-term memory, rational/analytical abilities, and willpower. The subconscious mind contains long term memory, beliefs, values, imagination, intuition, emotions, habits, addictions, and self-preservation mechanisms. The conscious is estimated to be only 10% of the mind while the subconscious occupies 90% of it.

Psychic ability is said to be a power of the subconscious mind. Technically, psi information is *not* perceived through normal means, *not* arrived through logic, and *not* imposed by the willpower – thus, psi is not the forte of the conscious mind. However, your subconscious mind passes on the information to your conscious mind. It is not yet known how the subconscious can perceive and project psi, but these are some theories:

The subconscious is connected to a collective mind. Some scientists have theorized that individual minds are connected in a group mind – perhaps what Carl Jung called the collective unconscious. This enables the passing on of information between people, even if they're far away from each other.

Quanta contain information that may be retrieved by the mind. Quantum mechanics postulate that everything is composed of fundamental building blocks of energy called quanta. These vibrate at a very unique frequency and leave imprints on the space they occupy. Because of this, information can be gathered from the energy trails of an object even if it's not present anymore.

Everything is linked via 'strings' at a subatomic level. According to the string theory in theoretical physics, strings are even smaller building blocks that make up quanta. In this theory, there is no such thing as empty space, and everything is connected to each other via these very tiny energy strings. This makes it possible for information transfers of great distances. Normally, the conscious mind cannot perceive these subtle energies because of its limited scope, but with the help of the subconscious, it can.

Time, distance, and basically everything is an illusion. Some scientists, mathematicians, philosophers, and mystics have proposed that everything is illusory, and all that we know and experience is a delusion that we share in our conscious minds. There is even a theory that the universe is a holographic simulation, and scientists are presently finding ways to test its validity. If this was true, everything and everyone is a part of a 'reality' where limitations of distance and time do not actually exist.

These are just theories of how psi functions; they may be true or false, we are not sure as of now. What's important is that you believe that psi is real and that you can learn to work with it. Because you're using your mind in psychic activities, whatever is in your mind will affect how you receive psi. If you have doubts, take care of them. Research more and see credible psychics in action. The fewer your doubts, the lesser resistance you will have to psi.

The Importance of Relaxation for Activating the Third Eye

Relaxing is an effective way to encourage the production of alpha and theta brainwaves. It switches your focus from conscious to subconscious functioning. This is very important; if you don't make the switch, you will end up creating projections of expectations, fears, desires, and memories instead of genuinely perceiving psi information.

Remember: the conscious mind wants to be in the driver's seat, especially because it is the center of the will. This is why you should refrain from wanting to control results. You, as your conscious mind, should wait for what your subconscious mind brings to you. Do not force it to work in a certain way. You will only create your own fantasies if you do so.

Relaxation Methods

Slowing down your brainwaves involves lessening the amount of stimuli you experience. This means the following:

1. Decreasing sensory input
2. Calming down turbulent emotions
3. Clearing your mind

Physical Relaxation

Closing your eyes slows down brain frequency. It will be helpful if you have your eyes closed as you reach your psychic level and when you are using your psychic faculties. However, if you've already mastered maintaining the psychic level, you may leave your eyes open.

Being in a silent and dimly-lit or dark room is suitable for practicing psychic exercises. If you can't find one, you can practice where you are for as long as you can tune out light, noise, and other distracting sensations.

Take deep breaths – doing this will trigger a relaxation response in the body. Assume a comfortable position that will not allow you to fall asleep, such as sitting straight in a chair or cross-legged on the floor. Take a moment to observe how you are physically feeling. Attend to any aches and muscular strains. Make every part of your body relax as much as you can.

Emotional relaxation

As mentioned previously, you need to be as calm as possible so that you can go away from the beta level and receive psi information without contaminating it with your feelings. Deep breaths can also calm intense emotions, so keep on breathing deeply and evenly while intending to feel peaceful.

Release your worries and wishes for a while. If you want, you can write down what you feel and what you think so you can get it out of your system. You may imagine your emotions as sights or sounds, then manipulate them so that they become less intrusive. For example, you may see your fear as a black smoke within your chest – blow this out of your body with every exhalation. You may also say an affirmation such as "Every moment makes me calmer and calmer."

Mental relaxation

You can do one or more of the following to be mentally relaxed: bring into mind a tranquil scene, focus on a simple target such as a mantra or a countdown of numbers (ex. 100 to 1), or visualize your concerns passing through your mind like clouds disappearing over the horizon. Again, you don't have to strain yourself in making things appear into your awareness. Relax yourself and the rest will follow.

Good times to practice are as you are waking up, or just before sleeping because alpha and theta brainwaves may still be present. Try not to fall asleep; set your alarm so you'll wake up if you do.

Initially, you will need plenty of practice before reaching alpha or theta. There will come a time when you can get there in only a few seconds when you decide to.

The next chapter will deal with training your psychic abilities. You don't need to do the psychic development activities daily, but it's important that you practice the relaxation exercises very often. This will make your mind get used to going into alpha or theta during your waking hours.

Stimulation

There are some individuals who reach an altered state of consciousness through stimulation rather than relaxation. If you're one of them, try the following methods.

Movement

Physical movements can broaden a person's focus and release it from mental blocks, since moving the body does not involve rationalization and analysis alone. If dancing, walking, or exercising puts you in a state of trance, do it. Practices such as qi-gong, tai-chi, and yoga are said to involve the manipulation of subtle energy; by doing these, you familiarize yourself with these forces as well.

Chants

Chants are said to contain vibrations that create particular effects. These are some chants for opening the third eye:

- Hmmm (exhaling with lips touching to make them vibrate)
- Thoh (said as toe)
- Om (said as ah-oh-mmm)
- Ong
- May

You can try other chants aside from this. If there is a word or a phrase that holds a special meaning for you, try it out.

Inhale deeply through your nose and hold your breath for a few seconds. Then, release your breath and intone the chant, stretching out the word over several seconds. Repeat this several times.

When you pronounce the words in a certain way, you will feel vibrations traveling from your mouth and jaw to the center of your forehead. These vibrations may activate your third eye.

Music

Certain types of music can help to induce trance: shamanic drum beats, Gregorian chants, trance, ambient and new age music, etc. The important thing is that the music contains extended rhythmic loops. Also, there are sounds that are engineered to create trance, such as binaural beats. These are usually listened to with earphones – different sounds play on each earpiece to temporarily distract the conscious mind and allow the subconscious to activate.

Visuals

You can gaze at something for long periods of time to achieve trance. Mandalas and yantras are visual works of art that are designed to bring your mind into a meditative state. You can also try staring at a point in the distance. Feel free to blink from time to time, but try your best not to lose sight of the target.

To improve your ability to see with your inner eye, stare at an object or a candle flame and close your eyes afterwards. Recreate everything you saw entirely in your mind. Do this several times.

Visualizations

It is believed that thoughts control energy, so what you imagine has real effects on the non-material plane. In experiments, visualizations are seen to improve psychic ability.

Visualize your third eye activating. You can imagine shining light unto it, make it glow from within your head, or see it as an actual eye opening on your forehead. You can have your own way of imagining it. What matters is your intention of opening your third eye.

Extending Your Senses

The third eye will function as an extension of the ordinary senses. In other words, it will perceive psi that is not necessarily an actual sight or a sound, but the information may be translated into a sensory impression. Other than that, the information may come as direct cognition – having knowledge about something that is not associated with the senses. Simply put, you just know it even if you didn't see or hear anything using your psychic senses.

Even if psi may come as plain knowledge, it's better if you strengthen your sensory capabilities because psi may arrive in sensory forms. The conscious mind has a limited attention so many things escape its notice. If you use your senses to the fullest, you will likewise be conscious of sensory psi.

Choose a sense to work on. Find targets in the environment. For example, if you selected eyesight, get an object and examine it thoroughly. Notice its colors and shades. Scan it for minute dents and bulges. Absorb its contours and the way the object contrasts with the background. As you do this, minimize thinking about what you're doing. Simply sense.

Do this exercise with your sight, hearing, smelling, touching, and tasting. Dedicate 10 minutes or more for this. After a few days of sensory expansion, you will begin to notice more and more things.

At anytime you feel ready, extend your senses beyond the physical realms. Try to perceive invisible energies: nature energy, emotional energy, the energy of a person, location, or concept, etc. You can be physically there with your target. You can look at pictures or listen to recordings. You may even just imagine experiencing the target. Keep a blank mind as you do this. Have the intention that you will sense the energies of your target. Pictures, sounds, and other sensations will manifest in your mind. These are likely to be psi information.

Chapter 4:
How to Use Your Third Eye

Practical methods of using and developing psychic abilities

You can use your third eye, ESP, or psychic abilities for a lot of things (see Chapter 1 under benefits of having an awakened third eye). Basically, you only have to do these things:

1. Have a specific topic, target, or question in mind

2. Bring yourself to the psychic level and keep yourself there until you're done

3. Wait for a response

4. Remember or record the response (via voice recording, drawings, or written notes)

5. Interpret the response

Having a Target

Define a target carefully– for example, the symbol that your telepathy partner is thinking of right at the moment of your practice, what the financial outcome of choosing an option will be, or the present health status of someone you care about. You must be specific about what you're interested in knowing. Set parameters and qualifiers. This will help avoid getting muddled answers. It might also help if you mentally tune in to your target – by writing down its name, visualizing a tube connecting it to you, or by saying that you are tuning in to that target.

Bringing yourself to the psychic level

You can bring yourself to a psychic mode with any of the suggested exercises in the previous chapter. A sign of being in this level is that you are very relaxed and almost as if you're about to drift to sleep.

Waiting for a response

You must do your best not to force things to happen; if you do, you will only create projections that have nothing to do with psi. Be extra careful with this! If you're in a hypnagogic state already, whatever you think about will manifest itself vividly to you. This will effectively block psi. To avoid this, you must be in a calm and receptive mode. Keep your mind blank. Silence your internal dialogue. Listen to the subconscious instead of demanding it to work. Wait for images to show themselves. Also, accept the possibility that you may not get anything at that moment. You absolutely must not force results because doing so defeats your purpose.

Recording your responses

Record your responses as they occur and without alterations. Psychic information may come quickly; express it just as quickly. Do not second-guess your impressions because you will stop the flow of information.

Interpret your responses

When you feel that the psi flow is done, you may now translate the information you have gathered. Clues that psi entry has ended are the following:

- You feel pressured in getting the results

- The impressions you obtain are suspiciously aligned to what you or your client wants or expects to perceive

- Your mind is blank regardless of waiting for a long time

Signs of genuine psi information are the following:

- Impressions that are sometimes surprising because they seem unrelated to whatever's in your mind or in the environment at that time

- Impressions that arrive in bursts and switch to other impressions without an apparent logical connection

- Abstract instead of literal. More often than not, psi is symbolic and composed of several layers of meaning. However, do not ignore clearly spoken messages and concrete images just because they are plain. Sometimes, what you see is what is actually there, such as in the case of remote viewing an object.

You need to do trial and error in interpreting psi information. It's because your subconscious mind has a different language than your conscious mind. You have to familiarize yourself with how it 'talks' by doing the following:

Use your psychic abilities as often as you can. Record what you perceive. Analyze the recorded impressions and compare them with real-world results. You might be able to spot that your subconscious regularly uses particular symbols for concepts. For example, trustworthiness in a person can be represented by an image of your long-time friend, a decrease of something is symbolized by low tide on a beach, or a metaphorical go signal is pictured as a traffic light signaling green or a no U-turn sign.

Aside from that, you can go to your psychic level and directly inquire your subconscious about what its symbols are. Ask it for its sign for beneficial and harmful, many and few, happiness, wealth, etc.

You can also draw from the results of your sensory-extending exercises (example, anger looks and feels like steam, etc.) Record all these translations in a psychic journal so you can refer to them later on.

Testing Your Third Eye

There is a lot of ways to test your psychic abilities. You may create your own psychic exercises to evaluate how your third eye works and hone its abilities. Make sure that you can confirm whether your perception is accurate or not; you can always try your abilities on targets that you have no way of checking in real life, but this will not give valuable feedback.

Here is a sample exercise for precognition:

Get 5 different objects and place them on a table between you and a partner. Instruct your partner to imagine what he/she will do with the objects. Let him/her write down the steps they plan on doing. Attempt to know his/her plans by going into alpha and waiting for the scenario to play out. Check your impressions with what he/she wrote down.

Another one for empathy:

Have a partner pick an emotion and experience it. Tune in to this person and notice any peculiar emotion in yourself. Compare what you felt with your partner's chosen emotion.

This is for remote viewing:

Ask your partner to bring a picture with him/her. Tell your partner not to show it to you until you're done. Enter your psychic level and record your impressions. Afterwards, look at the picture and see how well you did.

You can also use your psychic abilities in real life situations as well. As usual, record your experiences so you can learn from them.

Conclusion

Thank you again for downloading this book!

I hope this book was able to help you learn more about third eye awakening!

The next step is to put this information to use, and begin reaping the benefits of awakening your third eye!

Finally, if you enjoyed this book, please take the time to share your thoughts and post a review on Amazon. It'd be greatly appreciated!

Thank you and good luck!

www.ingramcontent.com/pod-product-compliance
Lightning Source LLC
LaVergne TN
LVHW021747060526
838200LV00052B/3526